Application of Aggregation to Improve Forecasting for Seasonal Demand Patterns

AUTHOR: DR (ER) OM PRAKASH

ACKNOWLEDGEMENTS

All praise to Almighty Allah for giving me the strength to complete this research.

ABSTRACT

Forecasting is an important business area and wide research has been published on this topic. Researchers are coming up with new approaches and combinations of existing techniques are also being explored to generate the accurate forecasts. Rapid developments in technology are also helping researchers to explore the combinations of different forecasting methods.

The aim of this research is to study the application of temporal aggregation on seasonal demand patterns. Therefore the focus of this research was to analyse whether temporal aggregation can be used to smooth the seasonal demand patterns and hence simple exponential smoothing method can be used instead of triple exponential method.

In order to achieve this aim the author has explored the literature and prior studies around the topic. Critical review of literature enabled the author to identify the gaps that temporal aggregation has not been studied in the context of eliminating seasonal demand patterns and then using simple forecasting methods.

To address these gaps, the author conducted primary research which was mainly quantitative as the empirical investigation was done using statistical and computational models. The Visual Basic for Applications (VBA) was used to develop the model which implemented the functionality to aggregate data. The model also implemented the simple exponential smoothing method and triple exponential smoothing method in order to conduct the required tests for analysis.

The research found that temporal aggregation has the potential to smooth the seasonal demand patterns as results were better than disaggregated data. The research also found that data should be aggregated if coefficient of variance decreases, this would give better forecasts. The simple exponential smoothing method also outperformed the triple exponential smoothing method when data was aggregated. Thus triple exponential smoothing method should not be automatically considered best approach to forecast for seasonal demand patterns.

TABLE OF CONTENTS

LIST OF TABLES

LIST OF ACRONYMS AND ABBREVIATIONS

AR	Average Error
GMRAE	Geometric Mean Relative Absolute Error
HW	Holt Winter's
MAD	Mean Absolute Deviation
MAPE	Mean Absolute Percentage Error
MASE	Mean Absolute Scaled Error
MdAPE	Median Absolute Percentage Error
MdRAE	Median Relative Absolute Error
MSE	Mean Squared Error
PB	Percentage Better
RMSE	Root Mean Squared Error
sARIMA	Seasonal Auto Regressive Integrated Moving Average
SBA	Syntetos-Boylan Approximation
SES	Single Exponential Smoothing
sMAPE	Symmetric Mean Absolute Percentage Error
sMdMAPE	Symmetric Median Mean Absolute Percentage Error
VBA	Visual Basic for Applications

Chapter 1

Introduction

An introduction of chosen research topic will be provided in this chapter. The short background around the topic of the research is given in the beginning of the chapter. Then the title of the research and after that the aim of the research, research question and objectives are discussed. The chapter then ends with the scope and outline of the research.

1.1 BACKGROUND

The change in our lifestyle is due to the effects of the developments in the last century. The development and advancement in the technology has completely changed the way people were living in the early decades of the previous century. This development where made our lives easy; has also created many challenges for us. It has not only transformed our life but has also altered the way businesses were doing their activities. The production, sales, marketing, financing, and each and every function of the organization have been affected by the technological advancements and much of the credit goes to the computer or digital systems.

The competition has increased many folds and thus everyday new programmes and models are being developed by the companies which help them to perform different important tasks in conducting the businesses. Therefore, the need for the accurate and precise forecasts of the future trends is getting more and more important as decisions about many other areas depends on it.

The organisations take decisions in advance in order to satisfy the customer demand. Future is uncertain so an accurate estimate is necessary. The more accurate estimates helps organisations to make better plans and take accurate decisions. Demand forecasting is the key to planning and strategic decisions as their accuracy has a large impact on profitability and productivity of an organisation.

Organisations need demand forecasting at various levels ranging from strategic decision making to operational control. Inventory is one of the most important assets which attract considerable investment as they are the life line of any retail organisation. The costs associated with inventory make significant portion of costs of running businesses. Excessive inventory can lead to increase in the holding and opportunity costs whereas too little may lead to loss of sales (Summers, 1998). In both situations the ultimate result would be the reduction in profits which is the main purpose of any business. In this scenario accurate demand forecasting can help to set the inventory in such a way that profit maximisation can be achieved while minimising the inventory costs. Thus the selection of appropriate forecasting methods is critical in this regard.

Therefore, the author has selected to research on the forecasting methods with special focus on the temporal aggregation for seasonal demand. Thus the title of the research undertaken is:

1.2 TITLE OF RESEARCH

> "Application of Aggregation to Improve Forecasting
> for Seasonal Demand Patterns".

In order to forecast, the pattern of product demand needs to be observed first before the application a forecasting method. This pattern may exhibit different characteristics and seasonality is one of them. Many products may exhibit seasonal demand patterns due to their need by the consumer at certain times of the year, month or even a week (Kumar and Suresh, 2008). The forecasting for such seasonal products can be done using different methods e.g. Holt-Winter's exponential smoothing method and sARIMA (Ragsdale, 2008).

Exponential smoothing methods depend upon smoothing parameter selection which then helps to identify the trend and seasonality in the time series. Holt-Winter method needs three parameters and makes the process difficult. To avoid from using complex methods an approach can be developed through the application of temporal aggregation. Such aggregation reduces the seasonality in the data and simple exponential smoothing method can be applied instead of complex Holt-Winter method. Hence the author has chosen to do the research on the application of temporal aggregation to seasonal demand patterns and its effect on forecast performance.

This dissertation details a study of how application of temporal aggregation and different forecasting methods help an organisation to improve forecasting accuracy of seasonal demand which can ultimately be utilised for inventory planning and control. In order to conduct this research and to meet its requirements following research aim, question and objectives has been set.

1.3 RESEARCH AIM, QUESTION AND OBJECTIVES

1.3.1 RESEARCH AIM

To study the impact of temporal aggregation on forecasting performance of exponential smoothing methods in case of seasonal demand patterns.

1.3.2 RESEARCH QUESTION

The central question in this dissertation is can aggregation improve the performance of exponential smoothing forecasting methods. This main question can further be divided into the following questions:

1. What is potential accuracy improvement that can be achieved by the temporal aggregation of seasonal demand patterns?
2. Can temporal aggregation help forecasters use simple exponential smoothing method rather than complex exponential smoothing methods?

1.3.3 RESEARCH OBJECTIVE

1. To analyse the different exponential smoothing methods
2. To critically examine the role of temporal aggregation when used for forecasting
3. To identify the accuracy measures which can be used to compare the performance of forecasting methods with and without aggregation.
4. Develop model for forecasting of seasonal data through temporal aggregation.

1.4 SCOPE OF THE RESEARCH

The subject of forecasting coupled with aggregation is very wide. This research is limited to the one class of forecasting methods which is exponential smoothing and application of temporal aggregation only.

1.5 OUTLINE OF RESEARCH

The structure of this research is organised as follows. The research begins with introduction in the first chapter. The second chapter reviews the literature on exponential smoothing methods, aggregation, seasonal demands and accuracy measures. Third chapter provides the relevant research methodologies and approaches used in conducting this research. Chapter four gives the details regarding the forecasting methods and explains the developed model. Then the fifth chapter presents the results and findings of research along with analysis of the data and in the last chapter conclusion and directions for further research are given.

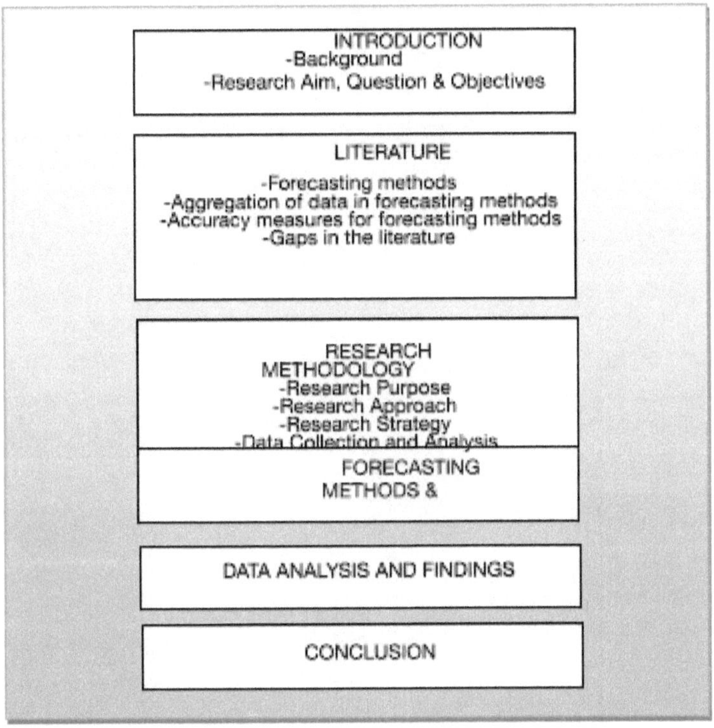
INTRODUCTION
-Background
-Research Aim, Question & Objectives
LITERATURE
-Forecasting methods
-Aggregation of data in forecasting methods
-Accuracy measures for forecasting methods
-Gaps in the literature
RESEARCH
METHODOLOGY
-Research Purpose
-Research Approach
-Research Strategy
-Data Collection and Analysis
FORECASTING
METHODS &
DATA ANALYSIS AND FINDINGS
CONCLUSION

CHAPTER 2

LITERATURE REVIEW

Literature Review

This chapter deals with any relevant work previously conducted by other researchers on the topic of study in different times. The following main areas of literature are reviewed in this section

1. Forecasting methods available for seasonal forecast
2. Aggregation of data in forecasting methods
3. Accuracy measures for forecasting methods
4. Gaps in the literature

2.1 Forecasting Methods

It is necessary to understand the different methods available for forecasting before analysis of its role in the inventory control procedure. Forecasting methods are broadly divided into two broad categories qualitative and quantitative. According to DuBrin (2011), most of the strategic planning relies on the combination of both methods. A brief overview of these methods will be given in next section followed by the discussion about exponential smoothing methods which are the focus of this dissertation.

2.1.1 Qualitative Methods

Qualitative methods are based on judgements, opinions, intuitions emotions or personal experience (DuBrin, 2011). They are subjective in nature and do not rely on rigorous mathematical calculations. Such methods can be used in the situations where historical data for the variables being forecasted are either unavailable or not applicable (Anderson *et al.*, 2012).s

2.1.2 Quantitative Methods

Quantitative methods are based on mathematical models and are objective in nature (DuBrin, 2011). The quantitative methods can be used in the situation when the information can be quantified and past data about the variable being forecasted is available (Anderson *et al.*, 2012).

Quantitative forecasting methods are Time Series Models and Associative Models. Time series forecasts project patterns which are identified in the recent time series observations (Stevenson, 2011). Times series techniques use historical data; some models attempt to smooth out the variations in historical data whereas some identify the patterns and extrapolate those patterns into the future (Stevenson, 2011).

2.1.3 TIME SERIES MODELS

According to Stevenson (2011), sequence of observations taken at regular intervals is called time series. Analysts identify the underlying behaviour of series by plotting the data and visually examining the plot. The data may exhibit one or more patterns such as trends, seasonal variations, cycles or variations around and average (Stevenson, 2011).

The naive and averaging methods are two approaches of time series models. Single previous value of time series forms the basis of naive forecast (Stevenson, 2011). Naive forecasts are usually used for stable series which has trend or seasonal variations.

The averaging methods tend to be more accurate than naive approach where random variation or noise exists in the data (Stevenson, 2011). The noise tends to obscure the systematic movements in the data (Anderson *et al.*, 2012). Averaging techniques smooth variations in the data and tend to remove any noise but in reality it is impossible to distinguish between random and real variations in the data (Anderson *et al.*, 2012).

2.2 EXPONENTIAL SMOOTHING METHODS

This section will provide the overview of literature and earlier work done regarding the methods available to forecast the demand of products. According to Tratar (2010), simple exponential smoothing, double exponential smoothing (Holt's linear trend method) and triple exponential smoothing method (Holt-Winters' seasonal method) are very commonly used for demand forecasting in a supply chain. The businesses have been using exponential smoothing methods for forecasting demand of inventories (Gardner, 1985). The success of exponential smoothing methods in different competitions reinforced their importance for analysis of time series (Armstrong and Lusk, 1983). Mentzer and Kahn (1995) conducted a survey of 207 forecasting executives which highlighted the fact that exponential smoothing methods are among the most commonly used methods of forecasting.

The single exponential smoothing (SES) method was developed in 1950. This method compute forecasts recursively and only need recent data point along with the most recent forecast (Brown, 1959). This was initially proposed as heuristic procedure for generating point predictions from historical time series data (Hyndman *et al.*, 1998). Exponential smoothing is a technique which is based on the recursive scheme in which the forecasts are updated for every new observation (Ragsdale, 2008).

Later on Holt and Winter developed double and triple exponential smoothing methods. The double exponential smoothing is an extension to the single exponential smoothing method and identifies trend in the data using two parameters. One parameter denotes the trend and other denotes the level of the series (Ord, 2004).

In 1960, Winter extended Holt's method to triple exponential smoothing method by introduction of another parameter which could handle the seasonality in the data (Chase, 2009). The HoltWinters method is useful for stock control when forecasts are required for large number of variables (Chatfield, 1978). According to Chatfield (1978), it is simple to automate and computer programs can be developed easily which can make forecasts without human intervention.

The Holt-Winter's method has two variations which depend upon nature of seasonal components. When seasonal variations are constant through the series additive method is used whereas multiplicative method is preferred when seasonal variations change proportionally to the level of series (Hyndman *et al.*, 1998).

Appropriate model selection is very important for accurate forecast as it has a significant influence on the forecast. Many forecasting models are available, thus to match the model with dataset is very important (Jain, 2006). According to Gardnar and McKenzie (1988), procedure for model selection has largely been ignored in the previous research. One approach to model selection could be the visual analysis by the forecaster i.e. analysis of data plot. But McKenzie (1984), Box and Jenkins (1976) identified that pure subjective analysis of time series is unsafe and selected model could have worse performance. Gardner and McKenzie (1985) developed a procedure for model selection for non-seasonal and depersonalized data. The procedure relies on three parameters. But the model was inefficient and complex for many time series (Gardner and McKenzie, 1988). As for constant time series, three parameters were to be computed where one was enough. In 1988, Gardner and McKenzie proposed a more simple approach based on comparison of variances of differences of data. These methods of selection were purely statistical. However Collopy and Armstrong (1992), developed procedure for selecting the best method which includes some rules based on observation of time series.

The implementation of exponential smoothing methods requires selection of smoothing coefficients and initialisation of values is also critical. Instead of arbitrary paramotor selection search algorithms can be used for this purpose. Excel Solver is good choice in this regard as demonstrated by Bowerman *et al.*, (2004). To find the minimum values of smoothing constants, search routines should be started from several points as the initialisation could impact the optimal smoothing constants (Farnum, 1992).

The exponential smoothing methods require that initial values should be fixed in some way as there are no means to generate forecast for them. Gardner (1985) presented some methods for initialisation. Broze and Mélard, (1990) gives the procedure to initialise all smoothing exponential methods. But empirical results for computational times are not available for these instructions, hence they are difficult to implement. More common approach to this problem is to take average of first few data observations and then use it as initial value (Ragsdale, 2008).

The outliers in the data affect the overall forecast. Exponential smoothing methods are sensitive to such data. The smoothed values are affected as they are dependent upon the past and current values of series which includes the outliers as well. Hence the forecast will tend to move away from the underlying trend (Gelper *et al.*, 2007). Also the outliers effect the selection of parameters as well. These parameters control the degree of smoothing and usually are chosen to minimise the mean squared errors (Armstrong, 2001). So in presence of outliers in the data, forecasts could be less accurate. In order to correct these problems of outliers Gelper *et al.*, (2007) developed an a robust forecasting method. The problem of outliers can be dealt by using Kalman filter for exponential smoothing methods as shown by Cipra and Hanzak, (2011).

2.3 FORECASTING THROUGH TEMPORAL AGGREGATION

Chen and Blue (2010) labelled demand aggregation as risk-pooling strategy. The reduction in demand fluctuation can be achieved through effective planning. In 2001, Armstrong has shown that forecasting accuracy can be improved through demand aggregation. Two types of aggregations have been discussed in the literature; Cross sectional aggregation and temporal aggregation (Maddala and Kim, 1999).

In temporal aggregation frequency of time series has been reduced by aggregating the data. The temporal aggregation of times series is being performed when sum of original data is done along the time dimension. Hence a high frequency time series is converted to a low frequency time series (Nikolopoulos *et al.*, 2011). Souza and Smith (2004), Amemiya and Wu (1972) tested forecast aggregation using ARIMA models which resulted in better forecasts (Tabar *et al.*, 2012). Whereas Rose (1977) showed that forecasts of aggregate ARIMA model were less accurate than those of disaggregate ARIMA models. In recent research, Nikolopoulos *et al.* (2011) and Babai *et al.* (2012) studied the results of different forecasting methods with aggregation and without aggregation. Both empirical studies focused on the intermittent demand patterns. Nikolopoulos *et al.* (2011) proposed aggregate-disaggregate intermittent demand approach. Different accuracy measures were used and the empirical results showed the improvements in forecast accuracy. The study was limited as it does not investigate the effects of temporal aggregation on inventory costs. Babai *et al.* (2012) extended this research and conducted another study to analyze the effects of temporal aggregation on inventory performance. They used three forecasting methods Croston, SES and SBA for the same dataset as used by Nikolopoulos et al. (2011).

The performance measures were inventory costs, volumes and cycle service levels. Babai *et al.* (2012) also validated that aggregation increased the performance for SES and Croston. But classical approach performs better in case of low cycle service levels.

Dekker *et al.* (2004) studied the use of aggregation in forecasting to improve the seasoanl demand forecasts. This study focuses on two concepts product aggregation and combined forecasts. The data from two wholesalers was used for this study. Holt-Winters' method and simple exponential method were used in this empirical study along with number of other forecasting methods. The results suggest that accuracy measures sMAPE, MAD and MSE decreased cosiderably when product aggregation and combined forecasts were used.

Another important research in the area of aggregation was published recently. The focus of this research was the formation of groups for seasonal indices and in which situation group seasonal indices methods peroform better than individual seasonal indices method. MSE was used as the target to minimise the forecast error and hence results were compared. The paper suggests that grouping of demand data can be used to generate competitive forecasts. The findings of this research are that aggregation and forecasting can be combined to generate better forecasts (Bolylan *et al.*, 2013).

The cross sectional aggregation is the aggregate of micro variables into macro variables (Maddala and Kim, 1999). The homogenous variables are combined. Top-down and bottomup approach are two types of cross sectional aggregation. The forecasting literature has looked at the comparative performance of these two approaches. In top-down approach the demand is aggregated before the forecast method is being applied at the aggregate level and then the forecast is disaggregated. In bottom-up approach, the individual forecast is produced first then the aggregate forecast is produced by combination of idividual forecasts (Armstrong, 2001).

The literature focuses on the comparison of bottom-up and top-down approaches. Zotteri *et al.* (2005) quoted difforent researchers (Theil, 1954; Grunfeld and Griliches, 1960; Ilmakunnas, 1990; Kahn, 1998; Lapide, 1998) who prefered top-down approach due to lower costs and greater accuracy. The lower costs are in terms of less forecasts at individual level. On the other hand (Orcutt et al., 1968; Zellner and Tobias, 2000; Weatherford et al., 2001) argued in favour of bottom-up approach due to the importance of demand patterns. When products have different seasonality patterns, it would be difficult to estimate the seasonality through top-down approach as information would be lost in this this. Also some authors took a different approach like Miller et al. (1976), Barnea and Lakonishok (1980) and Fliedner (1999) show that "forecast approach depends upon the degree of correlation and subaggregate forecast variables and upon the magnitude of correlation between forecast errors of subaggregate variables". These authors suggested that there is no one best way between bottom-up and approaches. It is depend upon the level at which forecast is desired.

2.4 SEASONALITY AND SEASONAL INDICES

Seasonality refers to the fluctuations in the demand of products. Changes in weather conditions, events in the year for example Christmas, can affect the demand of a product (Buxey, 2005). Seasonality can affect the social events, type of foods, fashion styles, and clothes (Roslow *et al.*, 2000). According to Pindyck and Rubinfeld, (1998) sometimes it is important to remove the fluctuations in the time series in order to view the underlying behaviour of the series. Different methods have been suggested in the literature which are mainly divided into two categories of Individual Seasonal Index (ISI) and Group Seasonal Index (GSI). As explained earlier Holt Winter's method can be used deseasonilise the data and then forecast can be generated on the basis of seasonal indices calculated through the method.

Dalhart (1974) presented the idea of estimating seasonality from the aggregate data. According to him all the data exhibit consistent underlying behaviour (Bolylan *et al.*, 2013). Withycombe (1989), mentioned by Boylean et al., (2013), believes that all products in line have same seasonal fluctuation. So in both cases assumptions were made that seasonal indices can be estimates in a better way if aggregation is used rather than the individual series. The earlier studies were related to the empirical research in this area where as theoretical foundation was lacking. Chen (2005) compared the methods theoretically and conditions are drawn in which one method can be preferred over other. Dekker *et al.*, (2004) and some other researchers compared the direct approach of deriving seasonal indices from disaggregate data with aggregate data. Since the scope of empirical research is too limited such conclusions cannot be applied generally. The conclusions differ across all such studies.

2.5 ACCURACY MEASURES

Accuracy measures are important part of this study as different measures would be used to compare the forecast accuracy. In this section different aspects of accuracy measures would be analysed as presented in the literature.

According to Hyndman and Koehler (2006), several accuracy measures has been proposed in the literature to assess the accuracy of forecast. In M-Competition (1982), several accuracy measures were used, the notable were Mean Absolute Percentage Error (MAPE), Mean Squared Error (MSE), Average Ranking (AR), Medians of Absolute Percentage Error (MdAPE) and Percentage Better (PB). Armstrong and Fildes (1995) suggested that any single measure of accuracy is not always best in order to evaluate forecasting methods. But it depends upon the nature of times series and the situations in which that measure has been evaluated.

MSE and MAPE were the primary measures of forecast accuracy in M-Competition (1982). However Armstrong and Collopy (1992) identified that MSE is not suitable error measure for comparison across different time series and forecasting methods as it is scale dependent. In later research Armstrong and Fildes (1995) also took the same view about MSE. Another significant error measure is Mean Absolute Percentage Error. It is scale independent and hence used frequently for comparison between different time series and forecasting methods (Frechtling, 2001). But MAPE is also not perfect and has its own flaws. When the series has which are values close or equal to zero, it gives infinite or undefined results (Hyndman *et al.*, 1998). According to Armstrong and Collopy (1992), MAPE has another disadvantage because It puts heavier positive errors are being penalised more than negative errors.

Fildes (1992), Armstrong and Collopy (1992) recommended MdRAE, GMRAE and MdAPE. The M3-Competetion was another important milestone in the research related to forecasting. Different accuracy measures were used MdRAE, sMdMAPE and sMAPE (Makridakis and Hibon, 2000). To overcome the problems of MAPE and MdAPE, symmetric measures were proposed by Makridakis in 1992. But Hyndman and Koehler (2006) recommended against the use of sMAPE as it places high as it still includes the division by numbers close to zero making the calculation unstable. The value of sMAPE can be negative as well which invalidates the term absolute percentage error.

Hyndman and Koehler (2006) proposed MASE as an alternative to MAPE and sMAPE. It compares error from a forecast model with the error resulting from a simple forecast method. It is scale independent and has seasonal variant as well which is more accurate than MAPE and sMAPE. But according to Hyndman (2006) it is somewhat complex than other measures.

2.6 GAPS IN LITERATURE

The above discussion of literature review shows that forecasting is very important for any organisation especially those operating as profit making companies. The empirical studies contributed lot to this field but still more concepts are emerging. The discussion shows us that:

- Researchers disagree on the application of any single method as every method performs differently in various conditions

- The field of aggregation has been explored but it is mainly limited to cross sectional approach.

Therefore by carefully exploring the published research, the author has identified that temporal aggregation has not been studied in the context of eliminating seasonality and then using simple exponential smoothing method instead of complex seasonal methods. So a primary research has been conducted to explore this area in depth.

CHAPTER 3

RESEARCH METHODOLOGY

Research Methodology

This chapter focuses on the overall methodology used in conducting this research. After the brief introduction it states the research purpose then approach, philosophy, methods and strategy of the research is explained. Then, it proceeds further by giving the information regarding data collection and analysis of the collected data. Finally, it provides the ways to implement validity, reliability together with the ethical standards maintained during the research process.

2.7 Introduction

The careful analysis of already present literature on the topic has depicted that there is not enough literature available on the use of temporal aggregation in forecasting seasonal demand pattern. Another notable point here is that literature on the current topic is unable to provide any particular research which illustrates: temporal aggregation can help to smooth the seasonal demand patterns and hence simple forecasting methods can be used. Hence, these mentioned gaps influence the author to carry out the research in this area.

Therefore, after conducting the comprehensive evaluation and critical review of already established literature around the topic, the author would like to present the devised methodology used to accomplish this research. The formulation of research methodology plays very crucial role in accurately attaining the objectives and also in getting answer of the research question precisely.

The research methodology in general is considered as the process of selecting strategy and mechanism for the collection and analysis of the data collected. Collis and Hussey (2003) defined that methodology includes the theoretical formulation of the research and analysis of the collected data; on the other hand methods are diverse available ways for the data collection and analysis in research process. Therefore, the detail discussion of research question, methodology and methods used in conducting the research are stated in the next sections.

2.8 Research Question

Can temporal aggregation improve the performance of exponential smoothing methods?

2.9 RESEARCH PURPOSE

Collis and Hussey (2003) categorised the research in four different types based on the purpose of the research. These are Exploratory Research, Descriptive Research, Analytical

Research and Predictive Research. These research techniques are not mutually exclusive but they are a matter of emphasis (Harvard, n.d.).

Exploratory research deals with discovery and building of theory. This involves conducting interviews, focus groups and literature search. The objective of exploratory research involves the identification of vital issues and variables (Collis and Hussey, 2003). It looks for the nature and of specific relationships. Descriptive research involves both qualitative and quantitative research methodologies. The descriptive research refers to the type of research question, its design, data collection and analysis that will be applied to a given topic (Harvard, n.d.). Analytical research is an exercise to explore the facts which are already available and analysing them to make critical evaluation of the information (Collis and Hussey, 2003). Predictive research deals with the situations when a baseline is given and finding what will happen. Usually such research involves some human behaviour or condition (Collis and Hussey, 2003).

The author in this research wished to identify the effect of temporal aggregation on the performance of exponential smoothing; therefore the author has applied statistical techniques and mathematical treatment on the data obtained. Hence, the study is categorised under the analytical and explanatory in its purpose as the research question was also accompanied by the hypothesis.

2.10 RESEARCH PHILOSOPHY

The research have not used qualitative approach as the focus is on the application of the scientific and mathematical techniques on the sales data to draw results and thus making the useful interpretation of the data collected (Bryman and Bell, 2007). Therefore as far as this research is concerned it comes under the paradigm of positivist. Positivist paradigm tends to generate hypothesis which can be tested and then it allows the author to explain the phenomenon comprehensively. This research has also generated the hypothesis which has been tested to explain the inter-relationship of the variables.

2.11 RESEARCH APPROACH

Moreover, this research has been based on the deductive approach as according to Bryman & Bell, (2007) it is assumed under the philosophy of the positivist. As this research starts with the theory and then the hypothesis were developed. Then those constructed hypothesis were tested with the empirical study and by the application of statistical methods therefore, moving from general to particular (Collis and Hussey, 2003).

2.12 RESEARCH STRATEGY

The strategy is another basis of classification of a research and this classification includes the qualitative and quantitative. There have been complex arguments about the issue that which strategy is better for research from the two Dawson (2002) but they both are good under particular circumstances and situations. Qualitative and quantitative both have strengths as well as weaknesses in their use. Bryman & Bell (2007) stated that the qualitative strategy is especially useful when the researchers tend to find the rich explanations and reasoning behind a complex complicated behavioural phenomenon, whereas quantitative strategy is uses the statistical methods and scientific tools for the analysis of the data.

Therefore, the current research used the quantitative research strategy. The selection of this strategy was also persuaded by the construction model which is using quantitative data. So the author has used number of different statistical tools to examine and analyse the data collected for the research. Thus the strategy used was perfectly suited according to the nature of this research.

2.13 Data Collection

The explanation provided above about the choice of the research philosophy, used approach and its strategy shown clearly that this research came under the continuum of quantitative research. Therefore, the author has conducted both secondary and primary research resulting in the collection of respective data specific to this research. The sub section below explains in detail the sources of secondary and primary data and also how they have been collected.

2.13.1 Secondary Research

Secondary research is also known as preliminary data gathering and is the exploration of the information for building up the understanding of the researcher around the area of the subject of research. Therefore, the secondary data used to assist and aid the process of understanding was obtained from the sources given below:

- Academic Journals- They are regarded as most authentic and reliable source of knowledge. These journals are used extensively to obtain up-to-date information and valid researches to comprehensively accomplish literature review around the topic e.g. International Journal of Forecasting and International Journal of Production Economies

- Books- Several relevant books have been used by the author to acquire knowledge around the selected topic area and for information on research methodology like:

Managerial Decision Modeling by Ragsdale, Business Research Methods by Bryman and Bell.

- Buckinghamshire New University e-Library- The University has provided this excellent tool to the students for accessing the hundreds of good e-books, journals and other materials. This helped the author immensely in gathering the useful information.

- Google Scholar- This one of the highly significant and authentic tool for accessing book and data to carry out research.

2.13.2   PRIMARY RESEARCH

The author has also conducted primary research for the purpose of answering the research question in order to achieve the set objectives and also to address the deficiency in the literature around the subject area. The primary data was made available to the author by a company X. The data consists of the actual sales figures of jewellery products of company X for couple of years.

2.14 SAMPLE SELECTION

The sampling methods can be classified in two main types which are probability and nonprobability. The probability sampling allows equal chances of selection for each member of the population whereas; in contrast the non-probability methods members from the given population are selected on non-random basis. Here, for the purpose of this research the probability sampling has been applied as any member of the population can buy jewellery of the company and hence became the source of increase and decrease in the sales of any day of any week and month and a year. Therefore, the author has relied on the fact that the data is actual sales of the company X during the last couple of years.

2.15 DATA ANALYSIS

The data analysis actually depends upon the selection of strategy of the research. Therefore, it is based on whether the research is quantitative or qualitative. The earlier discussion showed that the research is purely quantitative in nature therefore; the analysis will be done on the basis of the management science models.

The management science models used for the analysis includes: Single exponential smoothing, double exponential smoothing and Holt-Winter's method. In the first phase of the analysis these methods are applied on the data then in the second phase the temporal aggregation has been applied on the original data. In the third phase the three methods stated above has been applied again on the results obtained after temporal aggregation and then finally the results of the first phase are compared with the third phase to get to the final results of the research.

2.16 VALIDITY AND RELIABILITY

The authors of the academic research usually try to ensure that the two measures validity and reliability are utilized in their research to make them more credible. The validity is the measure of the fact that the outcomes of the research are accurately portraying what is occurring in actual reality in that particular situation. Whereas, reliability is referred as how dependable are the outcomes of the results are (Collis and Hussey, 2003). This means that the research is more reliable if the findings can be repeatable.

The discussion in the earlier sections of this chapter has shown that the research has been conducted to analyse if the temporal aggregation is suitable in forecasting for the company
X. Therefore, to maintain the validity and reliability in the research the data was collected in the real time over the years in a computerized system and no alterations are made on it, so that the outcomes exactly represent the actual scenario.

In the research author has also considered some other measures to maintain and improve the credibility of the research outcomes like there was no restriction in the selection of the data. Therefore, data throughout the year has been used for the research just ensuring the validity and reliability of the research.

2.17 RESEARCH ETHICS

In this research special attention has been given to maintain the professional ethical standards. The demand data was recorded by the company's computerized systems then it was provided to the author and thus the identity of the company has not been disclosed as per requirements of the company. This ensures the anonymity and confidentiality of the company (Dawson, 2002). The author kept the data of the company in a safe place and is not changed and tempered. It will also be made sure that the data and information should not be kept longer than necessary to comply with the Data Protection Act of 1998 (Dawson, 2002).

2.18 SUMMARY

The discussion by the author earlier in this chapter has shown the research methodology and methods utilised in accomplishing this research study. The author has used the quantitative research strategy with the deductive approach and is categorised as the positivist in nature. The data used for the purpose of this research has been obtained from a company X and has applied the single exponential smoothing and Holt-Winter's method along with the temporal aggregation technique to analyse the seasonal demand patterns. Special consideration has also been given to retain professional ethical standards from the beginning to the end.

Chapter 4

Forecasting Methods and Implementation

Forecasting Methods

The chapter would start with brief review of theoretical basics of forecasting methods used in the research and their implementation in excel. It is vital to explain forecasting techniques for understanding of results. Two forecasting methods Single Exponential Smoothing and Holt Winters were focus of this study. Hence first these would be explained then the accuracy measures and process of aggregation would be discussed. After that, implementation of these methods would be presented.

2.19 Single Exponential Smoothing

Single exponential smoothing was introduced by Brown in 1954. All previous observations contribute towards calculation of next forecast but the more weight is given to the most recent forecast because it is considered that recent history would show more accurate trend of demand. The past observations are given less weight. The smoothing constant is being used to determine the weight given to each observation. Mathematically equation can be written as:

$$F_{t+1} = \alpha D_t + (1 - \alpha)F_t \tag{4.1}$$

where

t is current time period

F_t is forecast value at time t

D_t is actual data t

α is smoothing constant, smoothing factor or smoothing coefficient and

Value of should be between 0 and 1. As the value approaches zero, the forecast is fully smoothed and curve is flat. Whereas when the value becomes 1, the series is not smoothed and most recent data point is retained in the forecast. The high value of α will have fast smoothing i.e. forecast will be highly responsive to the changes in the level of the series where as small value will result in slow smoothing i.e. sluggish response to the changes in the level of the series (Armstrong, 2001). The best value of α can be chosen by using different error measures. Mean Squared Error (MSE) can be used for this purpose. The value of α for which MSE is smallest can be used in the equation. A point of concern is the value of forecast when t is zero as previous forecast is required for the next forecast. Researchers recommended several solutions to solve this problem. A simple solution is the to use the first observations as starting point but a better approach is to use the average of first few observations.

According to Makridakis and Wheelwright (1977), this is only a theoretical concern which does not affect the overall results.

The exponential smoothing method is an approximation of moving averaging forecasting method. This model has an inherent drawback which is the failure to predict the recent trend changes and hence biased forecasts could distort the planning process. Hence the model would tend to underestimate the forecasts for products which have increasing trend whereas overestimate the trend for products which has decreasing demand in future. The method also cannot predict the seasonal changes (Armstrong, 2001).

2.20 HOLT-WINTER'S METHOD

To accommodate the drawbacks of single exponential smoothing method Holt introduced a model which can predict the trend in the data. But still the seasonal effects were not considered in the model. To overcome this difficulty Holt-Winter's method was developed which could be applied to the time series which exhibits trend and seasonal effects in the data. Holt Winter's method has two versions which are additive and multiplicative; in this study multiplicative method is being used.

The forecasting equations for this model are:

$$F_{t+n} = (E_t + nD_t)S_{t+n-p} \tag{4.2}$$

where

$$E_t = \alpha \, \frac{D_t}{S_{t-p}} + (1 - \alpha)\,(E_{t-1} + T_{t-1}) \tag{4.3}$$

$$T_t = \beta(E_t - E_{t+1}) + (1 - \beta)T_{t-1} \tag{4.4}$$

$$S_t = \gamma \, \frac{D_t}{E_t} + (1 - \gamma)S_{t-p} \tag{4.5}$$

Equation 4.2 can be used to forecast for time period t + 1 i.e. F_{t+1} by multiplying the expected base level at time period $t + n$ (given by $E_t + nD_t$) by the most recent estimate of the seasonality associated with this time period (given by S_{t+n-p}). The value of smoothing constants α (alpha), β (beta) and γ (gamma) in equations 4.3, 4.4 and 4.5 can be assumed between zero and one.

Equation 4.3 calculates the base level of the series, 4.4 gives us the trend whereas 4.5 helps to calculate the seasonal adjustments to the forecasts. The base level at time period

t (E_t) is updated in equation 4.3 by taking the weighted average of:

- $E_{t-1} + T_{t-1}$, is the base level at time period t before the actual value at time period t

- $S^{\overline{D}_{t-p}}{}^t$, at time period t it represents the deseasonalised estimate of the base level of

  time series

The seasonal adjustment factor calculated using equation 4.5 takes the weighted average of following values:

- S_{t-p}, represents the most recent seasonal index for the season in which time period t occurs

- $^{\overline{D}}E_t{}^t$, represents the estimate of seasonality associated with time period t after

  observing D_t

The estimates of initial values for base level, trend and seasonal effect are more difficult in this procedure. As a general rule, the initial values of model parameters can be set using historical data from first two seasons i.e. 2p to distinguish between trend and seasonality in the data. The smoothing constants in this formula are used for:

- **Alpha:** Alpha is used in all smoothing exponential methods. It acts as a data smoothing factor and determines how responsive a forecast is to sudden jumps and drops in the data. It is percentage weight in which more weight is given to the prior period and remaining is distributed to past observations in the time series.

- **Beta:** It determines the sensitivity of forecast to the trend. Less weight is given to trend in the series if it is smaller. The common approach is to give less value to beta as the trend is a long term effect.

- **Gamma:** In Holt Winter's method Gamma determines how sensitive the forecast is to seasonal factors in the series. If value of Gamma is less, the seasonal factors have less weight in the forecast.

2.21 Accuracy Measures

Several forecasting methods are available for time series. It is difficult to know in advance the best model for a given data set (Ragsdale, 2008). Thus a common approach is to model the time series using different forecasting methods and evaluate them to analyse how well they explain past behaviour of time series. Visual techniques e.g. graphs can be used to analyse the data. But quantitative measures are also available for such purposes. Mean Absolute Error (MAE) and Mean Square Error (MSE) and Mean Absolute Percentage Error (MAPE) are more common and recommended by the researchers as shown in the literature review. They also don't need complex formulation and easier to calculate. So these were used during the research by the author.

The formula for MAE is:

$$MAE = \frac{1}{n}\sum_{t=1}^{n}|D_t - F_t| \tag{4.6}$$

where is the actual observation

t is time period

D_t is actual observation at time period t

F_t is forecast at time period t and

n is total number of frequency of data

MAE is average of absolute errors between the actual observations and forecasts. The absolute of difference between actual observation and forecast is taken to eliminate the problem of cancelling out due to negative figures.

MSE is average of square of errors between actual observations and forecasts. The advantage of MSE is that it eliminates the cancelling out problem as all negative errors

$$MSE = \frac{1}{n}\sum_{t=1}^{n}(D_t - F_t)^2 \qquad (4.7)$$

have been squared. The formula for MSE is:
where all variables are same as explained earlier for MAE.

MSE is an accuracy measure which is difficult to interpret because it is expressed in units squared. So to accommodate that problem root mean squared error is used. Root Mean Squared Error (RMSE) is expressed in the same measurements as the actual observations and makes the task of comparison easy and more reliable. The formula for RMSE is:

$$RMSE = \sqrt{MSE} \qquad (4.8)$$

Mean Absolute Percentage Error (MAPE) is another useful accuracy measure as it is expressed in generic terms and permits the comparison between different lengths of data as mentioned in the literature review. So this accuracy measure was also used for comparison purposes. Formula for MAPE is:

$$MAPE = \frac{1}{n}\sum_{t=1}^{n}\left|\frac{D_t - F_t}{D_t}\right| \qquad (4.9)$$

But MAPE fails in the situations where actual observation is zero which results in undefined value. Also MAPE is zero when there is perfect fit but there is no restriction for upper level.

The values of alpha, beta and gamma for which MAE and MSE are minimum represent the optimal forecast for a given data set. Hence the generated forecast is considered final forecast.

2.22 TEMPORAL AGGREGATION

The high frequency time series are changed to low frequency time series, this phenomenon is known as temporal aggregation. As explained in the literature review, the aggregation of demand across the time series helps to minimise the effect of demand variability and hence improve the forecasting. Another purpose of temporal investigation is to reduce the zero observations. The author has used simple form of temporal aggregation in the research. This form can be shown mathematically by the following formula:

$$O_t = \sum_{} \qquad \qquad (4.10)$$

where t is the time period and

k can be obtained by $t + aggregate\ length.$

The equation 4.10 calculates new observation by adding original observations from current time period t to the observation k. The observations whose aggregate would be performed are not overlapping rather a one set of aggregation was calculated then another was calculated from the next available data. So observations do not overlap in aggregation. Aggregate length is the main control parameter which adds all the observations as specified by this parameter. For example if a time series consists of 24 observations and aggregate length is 4, then after using above formula the number of new observations would be 6. It would add first 4 observations then next 4 and so on.

Usually the control parameter i.e. aggregate length is set to quarter, half year or full year depending upon the frequency of available data.

2.23 SEASONAL INDICES

As explained in the literature seasonal behaviour is an important aspect of time series. Seasonality can be defined as the tendency of time series data to exhibit the same similar behaviour after some periods. Seasonality index of a particular period indicates that how much that period moves away from the average. To compute seasonality indices a full set of seasonal data is required.

2.24 IMPLEMENTATION OF MODEL

The analysis of data was done by implementation of forecasting methods in Microsoft Excel. The model was developed by the author to conduct different tests for final analysis. The author was interested in determining whether aggregation of data results in more accurate forecast, so accuracy measures explained above were also implemented in the model. The details about model development are being discussed in this section.

The technique to generate forecasts using excel model was straightforward. The model generates the forecasts without aggregation using single exponential smoothing method and Holt-Winter's method. The smoothing parameters were initialised to ensure the consistency and avoid from errors in the process. A macro to optimise these smoothing constants was written in visual basic for applications (VBA). In this macro Microsoft Excel's built in add-in Solver was used. The target for solver was to minimise MSE and change the value of smoothing constants hence getting the optimal value of smoothing constants.

Then the whole data is being aggregated by the model on another sheet. Again a macro was written using VBA for this purpose. The reason behind writing the macro is automation of aggregation process. The author specially addresses the task of handling aggregate length parameter. Any aggregate length can be selected and tests can be performed on the data. The macro was optimised for efficiency as reading and writing each data cell from excel is an expensive operation. This causes delays in the data processing which was witnessed during the tests. This problem was dealt by reading all data in single operation and writing it back in single operation after processing. The macro reads data into a single array and then processes it for aggregation.

Functions for accuracy measures were developed by the author in VBA. The functions were tested using different data sets for authenticity of the code. MAE function takes two parameters of which one is the data from original observation for a single product and the other parameter is the forecast for that product. Similarly other functions were developed as well for MSE and MAPE.

2.24.1 LIMITATIONS OF MODEL

The excel model developed in excel has some limitations due to the fact that author does not have strong background in coding a programming language. These limits do not affect the operation of forecasting methods and authenticity of results but they are related to the input of values. The code does not check whether aggregate length is greater than the number of observations of demand data. For example the data in this study consists of 34 months but when aggregate length of 50 is given, it is not being checked. The forecasting was generated and smoothing constants were optimised on the basis of Mean Squared Error (MSE), so it was hard coded in the code. But if smoothing constants were to be optimised for Mean Absolute Error (MAE), the change has to be made in the code rather than selecting it in the excel sheets.

2.25 SUMMARY

There are different categories of forecasting methods. Single exponential smoothing method and Holt Winter's method were explained in this chapter as they are focus of study. Accuracy measures MAE, MSE, RMSE and MAPE has been explained as well because these were used for comparison between different tests. Then the implementation of excel model was discussed in detail.

The next chapter will deal with data analysis, results and findings of different tests performed by the author.

CHAPTER 5

DATA ANALYSIS AND FINDINGS

Data Analysis and Findings

This chapter would start from the data analysis in which properties and characteristics of raw data would be discussed. Results of excel model and how those results were obtained would be presented here. To identify which method has performed better, results of each method would be compared against each other along with key findings.

1.1 Data Analysis

The dataset used in the study was provided by company X and has different properties along with some descriptive characteristics. It would be discussed in this section.

1.1.1 Data Quality

Data quality is very important element of time series. Data accuracy, validity, reliability and timeliness, relevance and completeness are some characteristics of data. Since the data was provided by the company so there were no means to judge these characteristics. But visual reading of data was done by the author and process of cleaning it for accurate results was performed.

1.1.2 Data Cleaning

Raw data always need some attention to analyse descriptive characteristics. Hence the author has only used data which could be useful in the research. Since data for lot of products was provided, the cleaning process was done. Following criteria was used during this process.

The first criterion was the length of time period for which data was available. A large dataset of products was provided. Some products has only 1 year data, some has 2 years where as the maximum time period was 34 months. Frequency of data was crucial for aggregation as data needed to be tested for different aggregate lengths. In such scenario data for 34 months was only selected for the tests whereas remaining was discarded. This was crucial as aggregation would have reduced the observations available and hence tests for SES and Holt Winter with aggregation would not be useful.

Then the remaining data with 34 months was further scrutinised. At the start of time series there were lot of observations which were zero for 9 months. These were also discarded as Holt Winter's method needed data of first 10 months to initialise the seasonal factor as less than that was giving error due to zero values. This would only leave 24 months data for analysis without aggregation. If aggregation would have been done for lengths of 2, 3 and

4, this would only leave 12, 8 and 4 observations respectively. Then Holt Winter's method would be useless in such situations. Also the seasonality of data would not be available to analyse the results. Hence after this carefully cleaning only 39 products were selected.

1.2 Data Characteristics

Dataset has quantitative characteristics as well. These can be useful to identify behaviour of data for analysis. Minimum (Min) value, maximum (Max) value, Average, Median, 25th percentile and 75th percentile has been calculated. First the average of these characteristics was calculated for each product then average of all those were calculated to get the single value. The statistical characteristics calculated for the entire data has been presented in the table. Along with disaggregated data, the characteristics of aggregated length of data have also been calculated to get idea about the changes in the data after aggregation.

Statistical Characteristics of Data				
Description	Disaggregated Data	Aggregate Length 2	Aggregate Length 3	Aggregate Length 4
Mean Min	11.17	44.44	55.10	84.77
Mean Max	174.51	268.26	337.85	424.31
Average	58.08	116.16	164.56	219.42
Mean Median	47.35	105.05	150.82	203.51
Mean 25th Percentile	33.60	76	108.98	150.79
Mean 75th Percentile	73.54	135.56	199.87	258.69
Coefficient of Variation	0.65	0.53	0.50	0.50

Table 5-1

The above data shows different characteristics. The mean of maximum values is high as compared to the mean median of 47.35 and average 58.08. This shows that most of the data lies in between min and median values as median is lower than average. Another indication is the 25th percentile which is quite close to the median. The 75th percentile is also low as compared to the max value. The max value shows that some products have high demand or there are outliers in the data.

1.3 RESULTS AND FINDINGS

The results and findings of tests will be discussed along with the procedure for tests conducted to collect the data. Two different types of tests were done for analysis. The main tests can be divided into two categories. In one category one smoothing coefficient was used for whole data set whereas in other category separate smoothing coefficients were used for each product.

1.3.1 TESTS CATEGORY 1

These tests were performed for whole data. Only one smoothing constant was used for whole data set. Test results and analysis for each method would be presented in next section.

1.3.1.1 SINGLE EXPONENTIAL SMOOTHING

First forecasts for disaggregated demand data were generated using the excel model. Initial values were calculated using average of first three months only due to less number of observations in the dataset. MAE, MSE and MAPE were calculated for each product. Then average of all MAE, MSE and MAPE was calculated. This gives us one MAE, one MSE and MAPE for whole data. The initial value for smoothing constant alpha was set to 0.4.

Similar procedure was used for aggregated demand as well. Tests for aggregate lengths of 2, 3 and 4 were performed separately. Again the initial values were calculated using average of first three months. Since data was aggregated, so the scale of units was changed which cannot be compared with results of disaggregated tests. To overcome this problem final mean of MAE was divided by aggregate length. Similarly final result of MSE was divided by square of aggregate length in order to compare like with like. Then RMSE was calculated from the final MSE.

Then these values were optimised for whole set of data. Smoothing constant was optimised to obtain minimum value of MSE. Only one smoothing constant was used for all products. The results for disaggregated and aggregated demand are given in the table 5.2. The disaggregated data has been referred as 1 in the table as length is not changed.

Single Exponential Smoothing Errors				
Aggregated Length	MAE	MSE	RMSE	MAPE
1 (Disaggregated)	27.91	2488.52	49.89	115.37
2	24.54	2158.78	46.46	39.05
3	23.22	2037.19	45.14	30.70
4				

| | 23.88 | 1615.07 | 40.19 | 54.82 |

Table 5-2

Along with MSE, other error measures were also calculated which are presented in the table.

The MAE reduced from 27.91 for disaggregated data to 23.22 for aggregate length of 3. This error reduced by 20% (27.91-23.22)/23.22. But then it increased to 23.88 for aggregate length 4. Though it is a minor increase but it suggests that more aggregate lengths would increase the error.

MSE which was the main criteria to optimise smoothing coefficient has decreased from 2488.52 for disaggregated data to 1615.07 which is a decrease of nearly 54%. But this fall in error has been notified for aggregate length of 4 rather than 3 as in case of MAE. The error only decreased by 22% up to aggregate length 3 but for aggregate length 4 it is more than double of it. Due to limitation of frequency of data available at hand, it was not possible to test the results for more aggregate lengths to identify whether MSE would decrease further or increases. RMSE has also decreased further as it is just square root of MSE.

MAPE is important measure of error as it is scale independent. Hence the errors can be compared for different data lengths as suggested by Frechtling (2001). MAPE has decreased considerably when the data was aggregated. The lowest error is for aggregate length 3 whereas it has increased for aggregate length 4.

Conclusion: The above results shows that all errors have reduced when data was agregated as compared to the disaggregated demand. This certainly establish that aggregation of seasonal data helps to achieve better results.

1.3.1.2 HOLT WINTER'S METHOD

First disaggregated demand data was used to generate the forecasts through Holt Winter's method. Since the data consists of monthly demand, seasonal indices were calculated for first 12 months and then Holt Winter's method was applied to remaining 22 observations. The initial values of smoothing constants alpha, beta and gamma were set to 0.4, 0.2 and
0.3 respectively.

Again only one set of smoothing constants was used for all products. MAE, MSE and MAPE were calculated for each product. Then average of all MAE, MSE and MAPE was calculated. This gives us one MAE, one MSE and one MAPE for whole data. This final value of MSE was used to optimise the smoothing coefficients.

Similar procedure was used for aggregated data. Tests were performed to collect the results for aggregate lengths of 2, 3 and 4. Since the data was being aggregated, the criterion for creating seasonal indices was also changed. For aggregate length 2, the observations for first two months were added then next two were added and in total 17 observations were available after aggregation. Following this, the seasonal indices were also calculated for first 6 observations as it corresponds to the aggregated data. The aggregate lengths of 3 and 4 reduced the number of observations to 12 and 9 respectively. In such case procedure for calculation of seasonal indices for Holt Winter's method was also changed. For aggregate length 3, the data has been converted to sum of quarters, so seasonal indices for first 4 observations were calculated. For aggregate length 4, seasonal indices of first 3 observations were calculated. This corresponds to the aggregated observations.

The results of Holt Winter Methods are presented in the table

Holt Winter's Method Errors				
Aggregated Length	MAE	MSE	RMSE	MAPE
1 (Disaggregated)	35.18	3221.79	56.76	101.46
2	27.94	2033.70	45.10	83.89
3	29.80	2901.10	53.86	73.77
4	31.13	2572.36	50.72	80.45

TABLE 5-3

Since MSE used for optimisation so first this will be discussed. It has decreased from 56.76 for disaggregated data to 45.10 which is reduction of nearly 25.85%. The aggregation length of 2 gives lowest MSE. But another interesting point here is that MSE increased for aggregate length 3 but reduced again for aggregate length 4.

Similarly MAE has reduced for aggregate length 2 whereas it increased again for aggregate length 3 and 4. It is showing different behaviour as it continues increasing for higher aggregate lengths.

Again due to change in length of data MAPE is more useful for comparison. Lowest MAPE has been observed for aggregate length 3. So Holt Winter's method has performed well for quarterly data. This shows that seasonal indices for quarterly data have positive impact on the forecast.

Conclusion: The errors for all aggregate lengths are lower than error of disaggregated demand data. This shows that aggregation of data is better and helps to achieve better forecasts.

1.3.1.3 COMPARISON OF SES AND HOLT WINTER'S METHOD

In last section individual results of SES and Holt Winter's were discussed, but now comparison of results in tables 5.2 and 5.3 will be done. Like to like would be compared against each other to identify whether SES with aggregation can outperform Holt Winter's method in case of seasonal data.

- **Disaggregated Data:** Single exponential smoothing method gives lower MSE, MAE and RMSE than Holt Winter's method but on the other hand MAPE is lower for Holt Winter's method. But still it shows that single exponential smoothing method performs better.

- **Aggregate Length 2:** MSE and RMSE are lower for Holt Winter's method whereas MAE is lower for SES. Here MAPE is lower for Holt Winter' s method. But since smoothing coefficients were optimised to minimise MSE so, in this case the author suggests Holt Winter's method performed slightly better than SES.

- **Aggregate Length 3:** All four error measures i.e. MSE, RMSE, MAE and MAPE are lower for single exponential smoothing methods.

- **Aggregate Length 4:** Once again all four error measures for Holt Winter's method arte higher. So in this situation SES has outperformed Holt Winter's method and gives better accuracy.

1.3.1.4 FINDINGS OF COMPARISON BETWEEN SES AND HW

Two findings of above analysis are important which are mentioned below:

- Performance of SES is better than HW in three cases whereas HW only give better results for aggregate length 2.

- When seasonal data is aggregated, the performance of SES and HW has increased as compared to the disaggregated data.

1.3.1.5 CONCLUSION OF TESTS CATEGORY 1

The above tests show that temporal aggregation has performed better for seasonal data and SES has outperformed Holt Winter's method. The temporal aggregation smoothed the data to the point that seasonal impact has been eliminated, so SES is performing better than Holt Winter in this case.

1.3.2 TESTS CATEGORY 2

These tests were performed for each product as accuracy measures at product level were minimised, whereas in tests category 1 accuracy measure for whole data set was minimised. Hence each product has its own smoothing constant which was optimised at the product level.

The results were collected at product level. The reason behind these tests was to collect more data for comparison between forecasting methods and impact of temporal aggregation on their performance. The results of MAE, MSE, RMSE and MAPE are given in Appendix A. These results were used to count how many times forecast with aggregate length performed better.

1.3.2.1 SINGLE EXPONENTIAL SMOOTHING

In this section results of single exponential smoothing will be discussed. The model was modified for these tests. Each product has its own smoothing constant which was optimised and hence results for lowest MSE were obtained. MAE, RMSE and MAPE were also calculated. In this section results of single exponential smoothing will be discussed.

A simple analysis in this scenario is the number of products which performed better for MAPE. This accuracy measure has been used because the data length has been changed due to aggregation. So to compare different data lengths MAPE is better accuracy measure than other measures.

MAPE - SES		
Aggregate Length	Number of Products	Percentage
1	3	7.69%
2	9	23.08%
3	25	64.10%
4	2	5.13%

TABLE 5-4

The above table shows that for disaggregated demand data, only 3 products has lowest MAPE than other aggregate lengths which is only 7.69% of 39 products. For aggregate length 2, only 9 products have lowest MAPE which is 23.08%. Whereas 25 i.e. 64.10% of products has lowest MAPE when compared with other aggregate lengths. And only 2 products have lowest MAPE for aggregate length 4. The above results show that aggregation has positive impact on data and lowest MAPE was achieved for aggregate length 3.

Conclusion: Hence aggregation of data is certainly a useful technique for seasonal products as the seasonal variation has been minimised due to aggregation.

1.3.2.2 HOLT WINTER'S METHOD

Now results of Holt Winter's method at product level will be discussed in this section. MSE was minimised for each product and each product has its own set of smoothing coefficients alpha, beta and gamma. Once again alpha, beta and gamma were set to 0.4,

0.2 and 0.3 for each product. Then these were optimised to obtain the minimum MSE.

Aggregate Length	Number of Products	Percentage
1	11	28.21%
2	4	10.26%
3	23	58.97%
4	1	2.56%

TABLE 5-5

Table 5.5 shows the number of products for which minimum MAPE was achieved. MSE is not being compared here due to the difference in length for disaggregated data and aggregate lengths of 2, 3 and 4.

According to above results, lowest MAPE was achieved for 11 products when demand was not aggregated. Then only 4 products have lowest MAPE when demand was aggregated for aggregate length 2. There are 23 products which gives lowest MAPE for aggregate length 3. And finally 1 product gives lowest MAPE for aggregate length 4.

Conclusion: In the above tests only number of products were counted for each aggregate length and it was found that forecasts of aggregated data have performed better than disaggregated data. It can also be interpreted from the results that one product may give lowest MAPE for SES for different aggregate length than in Holt Winter's method.

1.3.2.3 COMPARISON BETWEEN SES AND HOLT WINTER'S METHOD

In this section a comparison between two methods under study would be presented for this category of results. Similar procedures were used to obtain the results from different tests. SES will be compared against HW for disaggregated data, and then results of each aggregate length will be compared against HW. The criterion for comparison is MSE.

Performance of SES and HW at Product Level		
Aggregate Length	SES	HW
1	30	9
2	25	14
3	21	18
4	20	19

TABLE 5-6

- Disaggregated Data: Table 5.6 shows performance of SES and HW at product level. For 30 products SES performed better when data was not aggregated where as only 9 products has lowest MSE for HW method.

- Aggregate Length 2: In this category 25 products have lowest MSE while SES was used but HW performance has increased as compared to disaggregated data. 14 products have achieved better results for HW.

- Aggregate Length 3: Again the SES has performed better as 21 products have lower MSE as compared to the 18 products for HW.

- Aggregate Length 4: Once again SES is better as 20 products have lowest MSE whereas 19 products give better results when HW method was used.

It should be noted that this comparison is not between aggregate lengths but between forecasting methods. For comparison between aggregate lengths MAPE was used and analysis has been done in the previous sections.

1.3.2.4 FINDINGS OF COMPARISON BETWEEN SES AND HW

The above results show that SES performed better in case of all aggregate lengths testes. But another interesting point is that trend of SES is going down as the aggregate length is being increased. Though overall results of HW were good but its trend is going up. Testing for more aggregate length could reveal the situation whether the trend of decreasing performance for SES goes down and HW's increasing performance goes up.

1.3.2.5 COMPARISON OF MAPE FOR DIFFERENT AGGREGATE LENGTHS

For tests category 2 the minimum MSE was obtained at product level by optimisation of smoothing constants at product level. Then final MAPE, MSE and MAE were calculated by taking average of these measures. In this section the impact of aggregation in terms of percentage will be analysed. To compare different aggregate lengths MAPE would be used.

Aggregate Length	APE % at Product Level	
	SES	HW
1	122.46	295.14
2	35.54	60.66
3	27.60	43.14
4	48.61	80.59

TABLE 5-7

The above results show that performance of forecasting methods increased when data was aggregated. For aggregation length 3 the lowest MAPE was achieved. The percentage fall in MAPE is 343.69% i.e. (122.46-27.60)/27.60 for single exponential smoothing method.

Similarly the percentage fall in case of Holt Winter's method was huge which is 584.14%, (295.14-43.14)/43.14. Another important finding from the above 8 observations is that single exponential smoothing performed better overall.

1.4 Comparison with Earlier Studies

In this section the findings and conclusion of results would be analyzed in the light of previous researchers' studies.

The conclusion from earlier sections is that forecasting was better when data was aggregated. This confirms with the findings of Armstrong (2001). Forecasting methods also influence the performance of aggregation. Souza and Smith (2004) showed that forecast with aggregation using ARIMA models gives better results than disaggregated data. Babai *et al.* (2012) also conducted research for agggregation but with intermittent demand patterns. SES along with other forecasting methods were used. The author's findings corroborate with the findings of these studies that aggregation increase the performance of single exponential smoothing method.

1.5 REASON AGGREGATION PERFORMED BETTER

The above analysis has clearly stated that aggregation has performed better in nearly every test. But there must be some reason due to which forecasting for aggregation was better than disaggregation. To examine this coefficient of variation was calculated. The coefficient of variation is statistical measure and can be defined as the ratio of standard deviation to the mean. It is used to scale the variance of data in order to make effective comparisons. The coefficient of variation determines the variability of two or more series. The series of data for which coefficient of variation is large indicates that the group is more variable and it is less uniform. The coefficient of variation is unitless and allows to compare different data sets which cannot be compared otherwise. Coefficient of variation cannot be measured if mean is zero or it does not reflect the true picture if data has some negative values and misleads the analysts. In the current research the data does not have any negative value as product demand can only be zero or positive so it was easy to measure CV and then used in the comparison.

Aggregate Length	Coefficient of Variation
1	0.65
2	0.53
3	0.50
4	0.52

TABLE 5-8

The coefficient of variation (CV) has been calculated for disaggregated data. Then to analyse the results, coefficient of variation for each aggregate length i.e. 2, 3 and 4 was calculated. These calculations are mean of whole data as CV was calculated for each product and then mean of all CVs was calculated. The table shows that CV has decreased as the aggregate length increases. It indicates that data set is getting more stable. The effects of outliers and variability across the mean are getting eliminated due to which forecasts tend to be more accurate for aggregate length rather than disaggregated data.

1.6 CONCLUSION

The data analysis and findings have been given in detail in this chapter. The author analysed the performance of simple exponential smoothing and Holt Winter's method for different aggregate lengths. Findings from both categories of tests give same conclusions. Overall the results have shown that aggregation has positive impact on the performance of methods for seasonal data. The other important finding of the analysis is that SES smoothing gives us lowest MSE and MAPE in most of the results. The next chapter would conclude the dissertation by stating whether the research aims and objectives has been achieved and whether research questions have been answered.

CHAPTER 6

CONCLUSION

CONCLUSION

This chapter will sum up the whole research. First summary of results will be given. Then the research question, aims and objectives will be examined in the light of conclusion of this research. The recommendations and suggestions for future research will presented in the last section of this chapter.

2.1 CONCLUSION

Demand forecasting is crucial to any retailer, supplier and manufacturer. Forecasts of demand usually determine the quantities to be purchased or inventory to be held in hand. The retailers cannot wait for the demand to emerge and then order the products. They have to keep the reasonable stock in order to meet customer demand. That reasonable stock should be anticipated in advance as too much stock could result in the increase in inventory holding cost. Whereas too low stock can result in loss of sales and customers. So the best solution to avoid from these problems is to forecast the demand in advance on the basis of historical data. Forecasting procedures have been developed to solve these problems. Demand forecasting is a well studied topic and most techniques used in practice are relatively mature. But the researchers are still not clear which method would work in which situation. So the research is being done around different topic areas of forecasting. Instead of using one method at a time, the research about combining different methods is also underway. This motivates the author to conduct research around the topic of forecasting in order to understand the concepts in depth and how combination of different techniques affects the forecasting. The critical and comprehensive review of literature was conducted and following gaps emerged:

- The researchers are well aware of the concept of aggregation but most of the research has been done on the topic of cross sectional research. The research lacks in the area of temporal aggregation for seasonal products.
- The literature review lacks in research about eliminating seasonality through aggregation and also use of simple forecasting methods was not studied in detail.

Thus research was conducted to address these gaps. The research was focused on application of temporal aggregation on the disaggregated demand data and then single exponential smoothing method was used to forecast the one step ahead demand. Similarly Holt Winter's multiplicative method was used to forecast the demand for products which have seasonal patterns. The research was limited due to length of data frequency as aggregation restricted the author in identifying the trends and patterns.

The findings of this research have shown that better forecasts were generated with both methods of forecasting when demand data was aggregated. The tests were performed for different aggregate lengths and accuracy measures were lower for aggregated data. The research also concludes that single exponential smoothing method performed better than Holt Winter's method as errors were lowest for single exponential smoothing method.

The studies have been conducted by other authors about temporal aggregation and forecasting methods. But this research was unique in the context of comparison of disaggregation and aggregation for seasonal demands. And then performance of forecasting methods was compared in that context.

An interesting finding of this research is that errors can be reduced when MSE was minimised for each product hence getting better forecast for each product.

Now research aims, objectives and questions would be restated here to examine whether research was successful in achieving them.

Research Aim

To study the impact of temporal aggregation on forecasting performance of exponential smoothing methods in case of seasonal demand patterns.

Research Question

The central question in this dissertation is can aggregation improve the performance of exponential smoothing forecasting methods. This main question can further be divided into the following questions:

1. What is potential accuracy improvement that can be achieved by the temporal aggregation of seasonal demand patterns?
2. Can temporal aggregation help forecasters use simple exponential smoothing methods rather than complex exponential smoothing methods?

Research Objectives

1. To analyse the different exponential smoothing methods
2. To critically examine the role of temporal aggregation when used for forecasting
3. To identify the accuracy measures which can be used to compare the performance of forecasting methods with and without aggregation.
4. Develop model for forecasting of seasonal data through temporal aggregation.

The research aim depends upon the research question which in turn depends upon the research objectives set for the research. So starting from objectives, the author on the basis of results, findings and conclusions can clearly say that all stated objectives have been met.

The first objective has been achieved which is evident from the findings where comparison of methods was done and also implementation of methods in excel helped the author to understand the workings of exponential smoothing methods. The second objective has been met as well; the role of temporal aggregation was examined for different aggregate lengths and compared against disaggregated data which helped to present findings about the impact of temporal aggregation. The third objective was also met as all the findings were analysed using different accuracy measures. The fourth objective has also been achieved as model was developed in excel and forecasting methods were implemented to perform the required tests.

The research questions were answered successfully as well. The measure of difference between errors for disaggregated and aggregated demand, the comparison between MAPE of all aggregate lengths for test category 2 helps to answer the question about accuracy improvement. The temporal aggregation decreased the errors by 343% and 584% for SES and HW method respectively. The second research question was also answered successfully as conclusion derived from the results and findings of all tests favoured simple exponential smoothing method over Holt Winter's method.

The research aim was also achieved successfully as it is clearly linked to the research questions and objectives. The theory about temporal aggregation is confirmed by the findings as in the above discussion we have seen that temporal aggregation increase the performance of exponential smoothing methods as compared to disaggregated data. Also simple methods outperform the complex methods for particular aggregate lengths.

Thus, the research was successful in achieving its aim and objectives whereas answers to research questions were found as well. Now at the end recommendations and further research opportunities would be discussed.

2.2 Recommendation and Further Research

The author believes that outcome of this research is very useful. The findings of this empirical research would assist companies to decide about the forecasting methods to be used in management information systems. This research will also help companies to decide that aggregation is useful because daily and weekly data has been captured by big companies for each product. The data of products which shows monthly or seasonal behaviour could be aggregated and hence trend can be analysed accordingly. Forecasting for such products can be done on monthly and seasonal basis rather than on weekly and daily basis.

The potential extension to this research is to analyse data with more observations so that more aggregate lengths could be tested. Also double exponential smoothing method can be incorporated into the research to analyse behaviour of aggregation for products which only exhibit trend. The aggregation and forecasting is being done in two separate steps but further research could be on the topic to identify the methods which could help to incorporate aggregate length parameter into the forecasting methods. Also how to find best aggregate length and how it should be optimised can be the topic of further research.

BIBLIOGRAPHY

BIBLIOGRAPHY

Anderson, D.R., Sweeney, D.J., Williams, T.A., Camm, J.D. and Martin, K. (2012) *An Introduction to Management Science: Quantitative Approaches to Decision Making*. 13th ed.

Armstrong, J.S. and Collopy, F. (1992) Error Measures For Generalizing About Forecasting Methods: Empirical Comparisons. *International Journal of Forecasting* [Online]. **8** (1), pp.69-80. Available from:
http://repository.upenn.edu/cgi/viewcontent.cgi?article=1075&context=marketing_papers&seiredir=1&referer=http%3A%2F%2Fwww.google.co.uk%2Furl%3Fsa%3Dt%26rct%3Dj%26q%3Derror%2520measures%2520for%2520generalizing%2520about%2520forecasting%2520methods%253A%2 [Accessed: 2 February 2013].

Armstrong, J.S. and Fildes, R. (1995) On the Selection of Error Measures for Comparisons Among Forecasting Methods. *Journal of Forecasting* [Online]. **14** (1), pp.67-71. Available from: http://onlinelibrary.wiley.com/doi/10.1002/for.3980140106/abstract [Accessed: 1 February 2013].

Armstrong, J.S. and Lusk, E.J. (1983) The Accuracy of Alternative Extrapolation Models: Analysis of a Forecasting Competition Through Open Peer Review. *Journal of Forecasting* [Online]. **2** (3), pp.259-311. Available from: http://repository.upenn.edu/cgi/viewcontent.cgi?article=1085&context=marketing_papers [Accessed: 24 January 2013].

Armstrong, J.S. (ed.) (2001) *Principles of Forecasting: A Handbook for Researchers and Practitioners*.

Babai, M.Z., Ali, M.M. and Nikolopoulos, K. (2012) Impact of temporal aggregation on stock control performance of intermittent demand estimators: Empirical analysis. *Omega - The International Journal of Management Science* [Online]. **40** (6), pp.713-21. Available from: http://dx.doi.org/10.1016/j.omega.2011.09.004 [Accessed: 3 February 2013].

Bolylan, J., Chen, H., Mohammadipour, M. and Syntetos, A. (2013) Formation of seasonal groups and application of seasonal indices. *Journal of the Operational Research Society* [Online]. pp.1-15. Available from: doi:10.1057/jors.2012.126 [Accessed: 16 May 2013].

Bowerman, B.L., O'Connell, R. and Koehler, A. (2004) *Forecasting, Time series, and Regression*.

Brown, R.G. (1959) *Statistical forecasting for inventory control*. New York: McGraw-Hill.

Broze, L. and Mélard, G. (1990) Exponential smoothing: Estimation by Maximum Likelihood. *Journal of Forecasting* [Online]. **9** (5), pp.445-55. Available from: doi: 10.1002/for.3980090504 [Accessed: 20 April 2013].

Bryman, A. and Bell, E. (2007) *Business Research Methods*. 2nd ed.

Buxey, G. (2005) Aggregate planning for seasonal demand: reconciling theory with practice. *International Journal of Operations & Production Management* [Online]. **25** (11), pp.1083-100. Available from: http://dx.doi.org/10.1108/01443570510626907 [Accessed: 15 April 2013].

Chase, C. (2009) *Demand-Driven Forecasting: A Structured Approach to Forecasting*.

Chatfield, C. (1978) The Holt-Winters Forecasting Procedure. *Journal of the Royal Statistical Society. Series C (Applied Statistics)* [Online]. **27** (3), pp.264-79. Available from: http://www.jstor.org/stable/2347162 [Accessed: 20 January 2013].

Chen, A. and Blue, J. (2010) Performance analysis of demand planning approaches for aggregating, forecasting and disaggregating interrelated demands. *International Journal of Production Economics* [Online]. **128** (2), pp.586-602. Available from: http://dx.doi.org/10.1016/j.ijpe.2010.07.006 [Accessed: 03 February 2013].

Cipra, T. and Hanzak, T. (2011) Exponential Smoothing For Time Series With Outliers. *Kybernetika* [Online]. **47**, pp.165-78. Available from: http://www.kybernetika.cz/content/2011/2/165/paper.pdf [Accessed: 28 January 2013].

Collis, J. and Hussey, R. (2003) *Business Research : A Practical Guide For Undergraduate And Postgraduate Students*. [Ebook]. 2nd ed. eBook Collection EBSCOhost.

Collopy, F. and Armstrong, J.S. (1992) Rule-Based Forecasting: Development and Validation of an Expert Systems Approach to Combining Time Series Extrapolations. *Management Science* [Online]. **38** (10), pp.1394-414. Available from: http://www.jstor.org/stable/2632670 [Accessed: 27 January 2013].

Dawson, C. (2002) *Practical Research Methods: A User-friendly Guide to Mastering Research Techniques and Projects*. 1st ed.

Dekker, M., Donselaar, K.v. and Ouwehand, P. (2004) How to use aggregation and combined forecasting to improve seasonal demand forecasts. *International Journal of Production Economics* [Online]. **90** (2), pp.151-67. Available from: http://dx.doi.org/10.1016/j.ijpe.2004.02.004 [Accessed: 2 February 2013].

DuBrin, A.J. (2011) *Essentials of Management*. 9th ed.

Farnum, N.R. (1992) Exponential Smoothing: Behavior of the Ex-Post Sum of Squares near 0 and 1. *Journal of Forecasting* [Online]. **11** (1), p.47. Available from: http://search.proquest.com/docview/219159544?accountid=7179 [Accessed: 10 April 2013].

Frechtling, D.C. (2001) *Forecasting Tourism Demand: Methods and Strategies*. 1st ed.

Gardner, E.S. and McKenzie, E. (1988) Model Identification in Exponential Smoothing. *The Journal of the Operational Research Society* [Online]. **39** (9), pp.863-67. Available from: http://www.jstor.org/stable/2583529 [Accessed: 22 January 2013].

Gardner, E.S. (1985) Exponential Smoothing: The State of the Art. *Journal of Forecasting* [Online]. **4** (1), pp.1-28. Available from: EBSCOHost [Accessed: 25 January 2013].

Gelper, S., Fried, R. and Croux, C. (2007) *Robust Forecasting with Exponential and Holt-Winters Smoothing* [online]. Katholieke University. Available from: https://lirias.kuleuven.be/bitstream/123456789/120456/1/KBI_0718.pdf [Accessed: 21 February 2013].

Harvard (n.d.) *Research Methods: Some Notes to Orient You* [online]. HHarvard University. Available from: http://isites.harvard.edu/fs/docs/icb.topic851950.files/Research%20Methods_Some%20Notes.pdf [Accessed: 27 January 2013].

Hyndman, R.J. and Koehler, A.B. (2006) Another look at measures of forecast accuracy. *International Journal of Forecasting* [Online]. **22**(4), pp.679-6888. Available from: http://dx.doi.org/10.1016/j.ijforecast.2006.03.001 [Accessed: 31 January 2013].

Hyndman, R., Makridakis, S.G. and Wheelwright, S.C. (1998) *Forecasting: Methods and Applications*. 3rd ed.

Jain, C.L. (2006) Benchmarking Forecasting Errors. *Journal of Business Forecasting*. **25** (18), p.18. [Accessed: 27 April 2013].

Kumar, S.A. and Suresh, N. (2008) *Production and Operations Management*. [eBook]. 2nd ed. Available from: http://tn.upi.edu/pdf/Production_and_Operations_Management.pdf [Accessed: 5 February 2013].

Maddala, G.S. and Kim, I.-M. (1999) *Unit Roots, Cointegration, and Structural Change*. Reprinted ed.

Makridakis, S. and Hibon, M. (2000) The M3-Competition: results, conclusions and implications. *International Journal of Forecasting* [Online]. **16** (4), pp.451-76. Available from: http://dx.doi.org/10.1016/S0169-2070(00)00057-1 [Accessed: 2 February 2013].

Makridakis, S.G. and Wheelwright, S.C. (1977) *Forecasting Methods for Management*.

Muth, J.F. (1960) Optimal Properties of Exponentially Weighted Forecasts. *Journal of the American Statistical Association* [Online]. **55,** pp.299-306. Available from: http://www.jstor.org/stable/2281742 [Accessed: 25 January 2013].

Nikolopoulos, K., Syntetos, A., Boylan, J., Petropoulos, F. and Assimakopoulos, V. (2011) An aggregate– disaggregate intermittent demand approach (ADIDA) to forecasting: an empirical proposition and analysis. *Journal of the Operational Research Society* [Online]. **62** (3), pp.544-54. Available from: http://dx.doi.org/10.1057/jors.2010.32 [Accessed: 03 February 2013].

Ord, K. (2004) Charles Holt's report on exponentially weighted moving averages: an introduction and appreciation. *International Journal of Forecasting* [Online]. **20** (1), pp.1-3. Available from: http://dx.doi.org/10.1016/j.ijforecast.2003.09.016 [Accessed: 3 February 2013].

Pindyck, R.S. and Rubinfeld, D.L. (1998) *Econometric Models and Economic Forecasts*. Singapore: Irwin McGraw-Hill.

Ragsdale, C.T. (2008) *Managerial Decision Modeling*. International ed. ed.

Roslow, S., Li, T. and Nicholls, J.A.F. (2000) Impact of situational variables and demographic attributes in two seasons on purchase behaviour. *European Journal of Marketing* [Online]. **34** (9/10), pp.1167-
80. Available from: http://dx.doi.org/10.1108/03090560010342548 [Accessed: 7 April 2013].

Sbrana, G. and Silvestrini, A. (2010) *Aggregation of Exponential Smoothing Processes with an Application to Portforlio Risk Evaluation* [online]. Center for Operational Research and Econometrics. Available from: http://www.uclouvain.be/cps/ucl/doc/core/documents/coredp2010_39web.pdf [Accessed: 2 February 2013].

Stevenson, W.J. (2011) *Operations Management*. 11th ed.

Summers, M.R. (1998) *Analyzing Operations in Business: Issues, Tools, and Techniques*. 1st ed.

Tabar, B.R., Ducq, Y., Babai, M.Z. and Syntetos, A.A. (2012) *Forecasting Autoregressive Demands with Temporal Aggregation* [online]. HAL Archives. Available from: http://hal.archivesouvertes.fr/docs/00/72/85/74/PDF/paper_196.pdf [Accessed: 3 February 2013].

Tratar, L.F. (2010) Joint optimisation of demand forecasting and stock control parameters. *International Journal of Production Economics* [Online]. **127** (1), pp.173-79. Available from: http://dx.doi.org/10.1016/j.ijpe.2010.05.009 [Accessed: 20 January 2013].

Zotteri, G., Kalchschmidt, M. and Caniato, F. (2005) The impact of aggregation level on forecasting performance. *International Journal of Production Economics* [Online]. **93-94**, pp.479-91. Available from: http://dx.doi.org/10.1016/j.ijpe.2004.06.044 [Accessed: 3 February 2013].

3

APPENDICES

Appendix A - Product Level Errors

| | MAE SES | | |
SES	SES Aggregate Length 2	SES Aggregate Length 3	SES Aggregate Length 4
45.96	95.94	99.74	111.91
68.58	112.28	136.43	173.54
87.45	117.82	271.17	307.50
165.92	295.52	449.76	384.78
29.25	46.81	63.29	97.63
19.89	28.38	37.74	67.28
4.65	8.72	11.65	17.33
15.36	20.44	26.54	58.25
12.82	19.91	28.15	42.28
13.31	24.91	35.85	63.41
19.95	36.86	50.56	63.79
26.35	48.60	41.19	54.95
28.14	74.00	78.79	117.07
48.07	101.97	196.53	227.02
13.47	35.20	33.26	56.22
18.29	40.95	43.44	78.99
20.82	34.39	60.55	79.57
21.75	32.85	39.75	70.43
11.85	16.16	19.74	32.83
20.24	27.49	39.79	57.33
15.08	18.07	31.05	35.47
14.17	20.00	27.52	38.45
21.10	28.45	38.53	68.41
27.09	37.88	56.65	94.80
13.06	14.35	20.09	30.23
18.80	27.36	21.22	43.50
23.67	43.44	35.52	61.22
20.00	36.76	48.68	61.37
28.88	30.74	59.98	105.27
16.99	36.42	40.22	69.74
10.23	20.76	24.07	44.15
28.48	53.37	56.91	112.83
31.48	49.38	60.38	130.09
18.63	33.41	42.73	78.58
13.07	14.14	13.73	19.60